How to Get a

Six-Pack in Six Weeks

Schayaan Salim, Tyler Johnson, Brooke Goldin, Olivia Richards, Haylee Horton

DEDICATION

This book is dedicated to our devoted Biology and Anatomy and Physiology facilitator, Mrs. Kim Wootton. We couldn't have learned all of this information and made this book without her help.

CONTENTS

ACKNOWLEDGMENTS

We would also like to acknowledge Mrs. Kim Wootton again for helping us through the making of this book. We would also like to acknowledge the authors of articles and sources we used from the internet.

1 THE CHEMISTRY OF LIFE

Even though we don't notice it, chemistry controls everything we do. Chemistry is in what we eat, drink, and breathe. Chemistry is the science of matter. In order to get a six-pack in six weeks, knowledge of this branch of science is essential. Everything that happens in your body and the world around you is a product of certain chemical reactions. Although it may seem slightly intimidating to think about how chemistry controls our lives, living systems can be simplified into four major compounds: proteins, lipids, carbohydrates, and nucleic acids.

As you may know, chemistry affects a lot of our life. A big part of what it affects is the way we build muscles. Obviously, this is essential to getting a six-pack in six weeks. Therefore, the first compound you need to know about is

protein. Every cell in your body is made partially from protein. Proteins are made up of monopeptides, which are monomers, or in simplistic terms, building blocks. Each monopeptide has one amino acid, and there is a chain of 20 monopeptides in the primary level of a

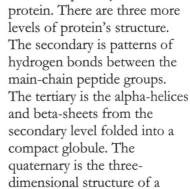

protein. There are three more levels of protein's structure. The secondary is patterns of hydrogen bonds between the main-chain peptide groups. The tertiary is the alpha-helices and beta-sheets from the secondary level folded into a compact globule. The quaternary is the three-dimensional structure of a multi-subunit protein and how the subunits fit together. Amino acids are also the building blocks of muscles. After you work out, your muscles need to rebuild, and protein is what rebuilds them. So, in order to build muscles and get that six-pack you've been wanting all of your life, YOU NEED TO EAT PROTEIN. There are many types of food you can eat to get that protein you need. Some examples are: eggs, lean meat, fish, milk, and nuts. You can also go on an alternative route and eat whey or soy protein powder mixed in with smoothies and other drinks. Without protein, you won't be able to build those essential muscles needed to have a defined six-pack.

The next big compound of life that you need to know about is carbohydrates. Carbohydrates are made up of carbon, hydrogen, and oxygen. The most basic unit of carbohydrates are monosaccharides, which are the simplest forms of sugar. Examples include glucose, fructose, galactose, and ribose. I'm sure that you've heard all bad things about carbs and that if you eat them you won't build muscle and become healthier. IT'S NOT TRUE. Well, it's partially true. There are

good carbs and bad carbs. Good carbs are complex, and it takes your body a longer amount of time to break them down into glucose. Some examples of these are: vegetables, fruits, whole grains, and beans. Bad carbs are refined and simple, and some examples of these are: white bread, cakes, and other foods containing added sugar. You may be asking now, why do I need good carbs, and why should I avoid the bad ones? Well, when the carbohydrates are broken down to monosaccharides, it gives your body the energy it needs to keep things going. These simple forms of sugar are a very useful source of energy for organisms. This is why many people eat food with complex carbs in them before they go work out. The reason you shouldn't eat the simple, or bad, carbohydrates is fairly self-explanatory. They filled with refined white grains and added sugars. These aren't healthy and can quickly increase your weight. So remember, for a six-pack, eat vegetables, fruit, whole grains, and beans before you work out so you have that energy you need to push yourself and build those muscles.

Lipids are the third compound that you need to know about if you want to get a six-pack in six weeks. Like carbohydrates, there are good and bad lipids. The two major types of lipids are saturated and unsaturated fats. Saturated fats are solid at room temperature and can be bad for your heart and health.

Examples of saturated fats are meat, dairy products, chips, and pastries. The chemical structure of a saturated fat is fully saturated with hydrogen atoms, and does not contain double bonds between carbon atoms. These fats are known to raise your LDL cholesterol. Unsaturated fats on the other hand have the ability to lower your LDL cholesterol and raise your HDL cholesterol. Unsaturated fats are found in nuts, olives, avocados, corn, and peanut oil. Cholesterol provides your body with energy and is used to make hormones and bile acids necessary to help digest food. Although it is made by the body, it can also be taken in by certain foods. It may seem like cholesterol is all good for you, but too much of it can lead to a buildup of plaque in your arteries, which can lead to heart disease or a stroke. Triglycerides are the other type of lipid, or fat, found in the body. Without physical activity, which you'll need for that six-pack, or being overweight, you can have high triglycerides which is can lead to becoming more overweight and less healthy. Just remember to watch your intake of fatty foods and you'll be on your way to that six-pack.

2 CELLS AND LIFE

Every single object, massive or miniscule, is made up of smaller things; Whether it's wood, screws, metal, bricks, cement or anything else that can serve as a structural or functional basis. Cells, the smallest unit of life, are the "building blocks" for every living being. Some are made many cells and some only have one. They all do different things to serve as the essential building blocks of the human body depending on how they're programmed. Some carry oxygen, others defend against invaders like viruses and bacteria, and then there are others that transmit signals. Understanding cells, their importance, and their function is vital in getting a six-pack in six weeks.

Before we get into what cells need to survive, we need to talk about the structure of different cells. Firstly, the two types of cells are prokaryotic, cells that lack a membrane-bound nucleus, and eukaryotic, cells that contain a nucleus. In prokaryotic cells, there are: the plasma membrane which serves as a diffusion barrier between the cell and its environment, the cell wall which is used for physical support, the nucleoid which is the center of the cell and contains most of the DNA, the ribosomes which make protein, and the cytoplasm which is a fluid substance that fills the interior of the cell. Eukaryotic cells are very similar to prokaryotic cells, but they also contain: the endoplasmic reticulum which helps to compartmentalize the cell and serves as routes for the transport of materials from one part of the cell to another, the vacuoles which contain enzymes, the Golgi bodies which process materials manufactured by the cell, then package those products into small structures called Golgi vesicles, the mitochondria which perform the aerobic portions of aerobic cellular respiration, and the nucleus which is a chamber specialized in DNA functions.

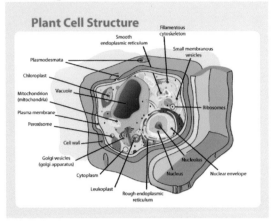

All cells require a certain environment to survive. Cells need nutrients such as water, oxygen, and protein. The cells can't survive or perform their respective jobs without these nutrients. When cells have everything they need to not just survive, but to thrive and fulfill all their jobs, the cell is at homeostasis. The dictionary defines homeostasis as "the tendency toward a relatively stable equilibrium between interdependent elements, esp. as maintained by physiological processes.", but in layman's terms it is just when everything is working normally and properly.

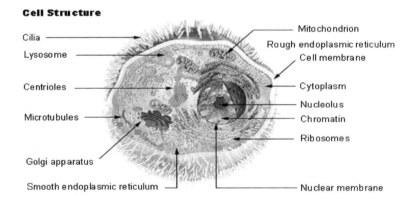

3 DIET AND WELLNESS

There's no question about it, eating right is a huge factor in getting six pack abs. Picking these foods can easily be achieved by learning the basics of nutrition. In order to get a six pack in six weeks, we have developed a few simple tips that are sure to help you fuel and nourish your body!

Pick the right carbohydrates:
Highly processed carbs like refined sugar, white rice, and white flower, have been stripped of a lot of their nutrients. That is why we call them "simple carbohydrates". These carbs are very quickly absorbed into the bloodstream after consumption. This causes blood sugar levels to spike and then fall low shortly after, creating an overall problem with energy levels. Most of the time, we are left craving more. The constant fluctuation stresses cells which is a problem that can lead to many different complications and will absolutely prevent you from getting the six pack abs that you want. Bottom line, stay away from simple carbs! Complex carbohydrates are the you want to indulge in. They take more time for the body to consume and break down. This allows glucose to be released into the bloodstream at a slower rate, steadying energy levels. With steadier glucose levels also comes hormonal balance and will steer your body away from insulin resistance. Complex carbs often come with a lot of fiber, which takes the stomach longer to process, leaving you feeling fuller which will help trim belly fat throughout your days. The following food items are great choices to consider when planning your six pack abs diet plan:

Food	Carbs per serving (grams)
Whole wheat products	8 - 12
Fruits and vegetables	5 - 9
Legumes	15 - 25

Pack on the Protein:
When trying to get the six pack abs look, your protein intake MUST be at a high. Protein will boost your metabolic rate, prevent lean muscle mass loss, and keep you from feeling hungry! Proteins are nutrients that are composed of amino acids which are necessary for proper function and growth of the human body. The following food items are great choices to consider when planning your six pack abs diet plan:

Food	Protein per serving (grams)	Other benefits
Chicken	7 grams per ounce (25% daily value)	- Rich in phosphorus - Contains a variety of B vitamins
Fish	7 grams per ounce (25% daily value)	- Full of essential fatty acids and Omega 3s
Beef	7 grams per ounce (25% daily value)	- Contains high levels of vitamin B-12, iron, and zinc
Eggs	2.8-3.5 grams per ounce (11% daily value)	- Natural vitamin D - Essential amino acids
Dairy Products	Varies in different foods products	- Contains calcium

4 EXERCISE AND WELLNESS

Exercise is the base for healthy living. There are numerous benefits to exercise; you will be happier, healthy, confident, more energetic, and will just look good. Going to the gym even once or twice a week will guarantee results if coupled with dieting. When working out, you want to push your body to its limits without. Every time you run, you should aim for a better time. Every time you lift, you should use more weight. Every time you do abs, you should do more reps. Working out makes your body more efficient and better at that task (faster, stronger, bigger), so to achieve the same amount of calories burned you must push yourself harder every time.

There are four main types of exercise; endurance/cardio, strength, balance, and flexibility. Using all four types of exercise will improve your overall health and looks, and reduce the risk of injuries. Endurance and cardio are the most common ones, these exercises are anything increases your overall fitness, health, and endurance. Some main examples of this are running and most sports, swimming, biking, and many others. Endurance and cardio exercises are going to burn the most calories and fat. Strength exercises are exercises that focus on building muscle. When doing a strength exercise you are actually tearing your muscle down, only to have it build back bigger and stronger. If available, having a whey protein shake shortly after a strength workout will help your muscles build back bigger and faster than normal. You can use expensive machines at your local gym for the most efficient results, but you'll see plenty of result at home with good old fashioned push ups and crunches. The third type of exercise is balance. These workouts focus on your balance and coordination, which helps immensely in sports and just life in general. You won't be able to impress that cute girl with your muscles if you keep falling on your face. The last type of exercise is flexibility. Being flexible is extremely important to being healthy. If you want your muscles to stay healthy, you have to take care of them. You must always stretch before and after a workout to keep your body limber as to not tear your muscles.

Workout Plan: Remember to stretch before and after every workout! Each week you should increase weight on strength exercises and achieve better times on endurance workouts.

Day	Workout	Repetitions	Exercise Type
Week 1:			
Monday	Freestyle Swim	1600 Meters	Endurance/Strength
	Plank	3 sets of 2 minutes	Strength
Tuesday	Bench Press	3 sets of 10	Strength
	Dumbbell Curl	5 sets of 10	Strength
	Barbell Shrug	5 sets of 10	Strength

	Crunches-Fast as Possible	50	Strength
Wednesday	Run	3 one miles	Endurance
	Bicycle Crunches	5 minutes	Strength
Thursday	Squats	3 sets of 10	Strength
	Calf Raises	60 Normal 60 Toes in 60 Toes out	Strength
	Leg Press	3 sets of 10	Strength
Friday	Run	3 Miles	Endurance
	Crunches-Fast as Possible	50	Strength
Saturday	Sport of Choice	1 hour	Endurance/Strength
Sunday	Rest		
Week 2:			
Monday	Freestyle Swim	1600 Meters	Endurance/Strength
	Plank	4 sets of 2 minutes	Strength
Tuesday	Bench Press	3 sets of 10	Strength
	Dumbbell Curl	5 sets of 10	Strength
	Barbell Shrug	5 sets of 10	Strength
	Crunches-Fast as Possible	75	Strength

Wednesday	Run	3 one miles	Endurance
	Bicycle Crunches	5 minutes	Strength
Thursday	Squats	3 sets of 10	Strength
	Calf Raises	60 Normal 60 Toes in 60 Toes out	Strength
	Leg Press	3 sets of 10	Strength
Friday	Run	3 Miles	Endurance
	Crunches- Fast as Possible	75	Strength
Saturday	Sport of Choice	1 hour	Endurance/Strength
Sunday	Rest		
Week 3:			
Monday	Freestyle Swim	1600 Meters	Endurance/Strength
	Plank	5 sets of 2 minutes	Strength
Tuesday	Bench Press	3 sets of 10	Strength
	Dumbbell Curl	5 sets of 10	Strength
	Barbell Shrug	5 sets of 10	Strength
	Crunches- Fast as Possible	100	Strength
Wednesday	Run	3 one miles	Endurance

	Bicycle Crunches	6 minutes	Strength
Thursday	Squats	3 sets of 10	Strength
	Calf Raises	70 Normal 70 Toes in 70 Toes out	Strength
	Leg Press	3 sets of 10	Strength
Friday	Run	3 Miles	Endurance
	Crunches-Fast as Possible	100	Strength
Saturday	Sport of Choice	1 hour	Endurance/Strength
Sunday	Rest		
Week 4:			
Monday	Freestyle Swim	1600 Meters	Endurance/Strength
	Plank	5 sets of 2 minutes	Strength
Tuesday	Bench Press	3 sets of 10	Strength
	Dumbbell Curl	5 sets of 10	Strength
	Barbell Shrug	5 sets of 10	Strength
	Crunches-Fast as Possible	125	Strength
Wednesday	Run	3 one miles	Endurance
	Bicycle Crunches	6 minutes	Strength
Thursday	Squats	3 sets of 10	Strength

	Calf Raises	70 Normal 70 Toes in 70 Toes out	Strength
	Leg Press	3 sets of 10	Strength
Friday	Run	3 Miles	Endurance
	Crunches-Fast as Possible	125	Strength
Saturday	Sport of Choice	1 hour	Endurance/Strength
Sunday	Rest		
Week 5:			
Monday	Freestyle Swim	1600 Meters	Endurance/Strength
	Plank	6 sets of 2 minutes	Strength
Tuesday	Bench Press	3 sets of 10	Strength
	Dumbbell Curl	5 sets of 10	Strength
	Barbell Shrug	5 sets of 10	Strength
	Crunches-Fast as Possible	150	Strength
Wednesday	Run	3 one miles	Endurance
	Bicycle Crunches	7 minutes	Strength
Thursday	Squats	3 sets of 10	Strength
	Calf Raises	80 Normal 80 Toes in 80 Toes out	Strength

	Leg Press	3 sets of 10	Strength
Friday	Run	3 Miles	Endurance
	Crunches-Fast as Possible	150	Strength
Saturday	Sport of Choice	1 hour	Endurance/Strength
Sunday	Rest		
Week 6:			
Monday	Freestyle Swim	1600 Meters	Endurance/Strength
	Plank	7 sets of 2 minutes	Strength
Tuesday	Bench Press	3 sets of 10	Strength
	Dumbbell Curl	5 sets of 10	Strength
	Barbell Shrug	5 sets of 10	Strength
	Crunches-Fast as Possible	175	Strength
Wednesday	Run	3 one miles	Endurance
	Bicycle Crunches	8 minutes	Strength
Thursday	Squats	3 sets of 10	Strength
	Calf Raises	90 Normal 90 Toes in 90 Toes out	Strength
	Leg Press	3 sets of 10	Strength
Friday	Run	4 Miles	Endurance

	Crunches-Fast as Possible	175	Strength
Saturday	Sport of Choice	1 hour	Endurance/Strength
Sunday	Rest		

5 PROBLEMS WITH NUTRITION

Unfortunately for some people in this world, there are deficiency diseases. These can affect anyone, even you! Because there are many problems with nutrition that people face, we'll discuss these in this chapter because it's essential for you to know if you want to get that six-pack in six weeks! Just remember to eat the different types of food in the last column so you don't fall ill to one of these deficiency diseases!

Vitamin Deficiency	Symptoms	Cure Foods
Vitamin A also known as Nyctalopia	Almost impossible to see in dim light and blind when it is dark	Carrots
Vitamin B5 also known as Paraesthesia	Numbing sensation	Avocados and Bran
Vitamin B12 also known as Hypocobalaminemia	Gradual deterioration of the spinal cord and very gradual brain deterioration, resulting in sensory or motor deficiencies	Meat, Dairy, and Eggs
Vitamin K	Risk of massive uncontrolled bleeding	Leafy Greens

Vitamin B2 also known as Ariboflavinosis	Cracked lips, throat swelling, bloodshot eyes, and low red blood cell count	Meat, Dairy, and Eggs
Vitamin D also known as Rickets	Muscles and bones become soft, which can cause permanent deformities	Fish (along with some help from the sun)
Vitamin C also known as Scurvy	Lethargy, skin spots, bleeding gums, loss of teeth, fever, and death	Guavas, Bell Peppers, and Oranges
Vitamin B7	Rashes, hair loss, anaemia, and mental conditions including hallucinations, drowsiness, and depression	Meat, Dairy, and Peanuts
Vitamin B3 also known as Pellagra	Diarrhea, dermatitis, dementia, and death	Meat
Vitamin B1 also known as Beriberi	Weight loss, body weakness and pain, brain damage, irregular heart rate, heart failure, and death	Fish, Dried Herbs, and Pistachios

CONCLUSION

We know that there is a lot of scientific information that you think isn't necessary for when you're working on getting your six-pack, but you need to remember that all of that information is important for you to know because it gives you that upper edge when working out and eating. The most important thing that you should take away though is that it's okay if you don't accomplish your goal of getting a six-pack in six weeks. It's not an easy thing to do, but as long as you work towards a goal and use this book to help, you'll be successful in your health and wellness. For more information and some motivational tweets, check out our twitter **@get_six**!

Works Cited

1. Will Eating More Protein Help Your Body Gain Muscle Faster?. (n.d.). *WebMD - Better information. Better health.*. Retrieved October 2, 2013, from http://www.webmd.com/fitness-exercise/news/20020529/will-eating-more-protein-help-your-body-gain-muscle-faster?page=21

2. Learn Your Lipids | Learn Your Lipids. (n.d.). *Learn Your Lipids | Know Your Cholesterol Levels*. Retrieved October 2, 2013, from http://www.learnyourlipids.com/lipids/

3. What is the Best Whey Protein?. (2012, August 17). *Renegade Dad*. Retrieved October 1, 2013, from www.renegadedad.net/what-is-the-best-whey-protein

4. Valenziano, C. (n.d.). The peerFit Group Exercise Blog: The Latest Trends & Tips. *Group Fitness & Instructor Reviews. Find a Class or Gym*. Retrieved October 2, 2013, from http://www.peerfit.com/blog/2013/08/red-meat-do-we-or-dont-we/

5. Fiber May Reduce Risk Of Disease, Help You Live Longer | Earth Eats - Indiana Public Media. (n.d.). *Indiana Public Media | News and Information, Music, Arts and Community Events from WFIU and WTIU*. Retrieved October 2, 2013, from http://indianapublicmedia.org/eartheats/fiber-live-longer/

6. Egg. (n.d.). *The Girl Who Ate Everything*. Retrieved October 1, 2013, from www.the-girl-who-ate-everything.com/wp-content/uploads/blogger/-94kdp4j_iyI/TakQNEB8RPI/AAAAAAAAGww/18tdRVqF9z0/s1600/hard-boiled-egg-1.JPG

ABOUT THE AUTHOR

Brooke Goldin is a senior at New Tech High @ Coppell. She lives in Valley Ranch with her parents, older brother and four pets. She plans to attend Tarleton State University in hopes of pursuing her dream of becoming an Orthodontist.

Olivia Richards is a senior, age 17, that goes to New Tech High @ Coppell. She lives in Coppell, Texas with her parents, and sister. When Olivia isn't at school, she spends time at her local church, at the gym, or with her family and friends. After high school Olivia would like to attend medical school with the future goal of becoming a neonatal nurse or OB/GYN.

Tyler Johnson is an 18 year old that goes to New Tech High @ Coppell. He lives in Coppell, Texas with his parents, brother, and dog. When Tyler isn't at school, he's either managing the Hackberry Creek Country Club Pool, playing and writing music, or hanging out with friends. After high school he is planning on attending Texas A&M university and earning a degree in Ocean Engineering. His goal is to work with marine biologists to produce tools to further explore the ocean.

Schayaan Salim is a 17 year old that goes to New Tech High @ Coppell. He lives in Coppell, Texas with his parents, brother, and sister. When Schayaan isn't at school, he's either working at the Coppell Aquatics and Recreation Center as a lifeguard, at home watching tv, or with his friends most likely playing football. After high school, he wants to go to the University of Texas at Austin or Texas A&M University. His goal is to go to law school and then become a lawyer after he's done with college.

Haylee is a 17 year old senior at New Tech High School @ Coppell. She lives in Lewisville, Texas with her parents, Robyn and James Horton, and younger brother, Hayden Horton. Haylee is a part of the Sports Medicine class and this is her fourth year participating. Her goal is to go either Oklahoma Baptist University or the University of North Texas and get a degree in Special Education. Her favorite sport is football and loves to teach children.

35867167R00020

Printed in Great Britain
by Amazon